Reviews from Business Leaders

"***Yes!* The Job is Mine** provides the job seeker with the required self-awareness to answer interview questions honestly and confidently to get the right job. It's an essential tool for the job search."

-Ted Powell, Managing Partner,
Stop at Nothing Leadership Development

"Terry has had tremendous success helping people discover their passions, interests and skills...while helping to match them to an ideal job and career. Her book simplifies and enhances the job search process so now everyone can be successful and find job happiness!"

- Patti Hughes, Founder,
CEO and Chief Creative Officer, Natural Life

"Terry Walton combines insight from years of executive search and interview experience to develop a job search process that works. It's an easy, 100-page book that produces results; I recommend it to everyone looking for a job."

-Rob Clements,
Chairman & CEO, EverBank

Yes! The Job is Mine
4 Steps to Get the Job

Executive Search and Career Coaching
advice to
Empower your Job Search

Terry Patrick Walton

ISBN: 1518764959
ISBN 13: 9781518764950

AUTHOR'S NOTE

How do I get the job?
What careers are good for me?
What skills do I have? How do I network?
How do I energize my job search?

I feel your pain! These concerns are real. They keep us from finding our best career and instead create doubt, stress and frustration.

"*Yes!* The Job is Mine" was written for you. It has proven solutions based on years of executive search, recruiting and career coaching experience. Designed for recent college graduates, mid-career job seekers, and experienced professionals, "*Yes!* The Job is Mine" provides fast, easy results; you'll find the answers to the career and job search hurdles that prevent you from moving forward.

Build confidence, knowledge and competence in all aspects of the job search: Self-Assessment, Resumes, Interviews, and Networking. "*Yes!* The Job is Mine" will provide you with the strategies you need to Power your Potential and find career happiness and success.

- - terry patrick walton

Table of Contents

STEP 1 –
Get to know yourself, your values, interests, and skills.

This Step is All About You –
How can you sell yourself for a job without knowing what you want, your strengths, your values and your interests?

What should I do?
What job is right for me?
What are my strengths?
Who am I??

Step 1 is the easiest way to get the answers- - and you'll know yourself really well by page 16.

Take Action:
Work through the upcoming pages to quickly get to know yourself….

My Passions and Interests

Review the list and circle Interests that are important to you; add your own if you'd like:

Astrology
Automobiles, Aviation, Boating
Biking
Business, Continuing Education
Cards, Board Games, Puzzles, Magic
Childcare and Development
Collecting
Community Service
Computer Games, Video
Current Events, Politics
Dancing
Do-it-Yourself Projects
Entertaining, Food, Cooking
Fashion, Interior Design
Fishing, Hunting
Fitness, Healthy Living
Friendships
Gardening, Nature
Horses; Animals
Movies, Television
Music, Singing, Performing
Martial Arts
New Technology
Art, Painting, Drawing, Crafts

Photography
Psychology
Reading
Social Media, Social Networking
Spiritual, Religion
Sports – playing, spectator
Travel
Video & Computer Games
Woodwork
Writing

Specifically, I enjoy:

____

____

____

____

____

My Personal and Work Values

Review the list and circle Values that are important to you, add your own if you'd like.

Achievement
Advancement
Adventure
Appreciation, Recognition
Beauty
Change, Variety
Commitment
Community
Competition
Knowledge
Creativity
Customer Satisfaction
Democracy
Discipline
Diversity
Efficiency
Equality
Faith
Family
Flexibility
Freedom
Fun, Humor, Friendships
Gratitude
Growth – personal or work
Hard Work
Helping Others
Honesty, Integrity
Ideas
Independence
Influence, Power, Status

Justice
Leadership
Life/Work Balance
Location
Love, Romance
Loyalty
Money, Profit
Moral Fulfillment
Order, Structure
Patriotism
Peace
Pleasure
Positive Outlook
Privacy
Problem Solving
Punctuality
Quality
Respect
Security
Spirituality
Stability, Predictability
Teamwork
Tolerance
Tradition
Trust
Working with people; animals

My Favorite Personal and Work Values:

____

____

____

____

____

Traits: "Things I know about Myself"

Review the lists and circle one phrase from each line that is **most** like you. Open up and be honest with yourself. This information (positive and even less than positive) helps determine jobs and work environments that will be best for you.

On each line, choose one from each column:

Ambitious, want more	Satisfied, content
Less Focused	Focused
Decisive	Indecisive
Structure	Flexibility
Specifics, details	Concepts, big picture
Cautious	Take a risk
Diplomatic	Straight Talker
Appreciative	Grateful
Work Hard	Work Smart
Perfectionist	Not Really
Punctual	Sometimes late
Enjoy crowds	Crowds exhaust me
To Do List	What list?
Motivate myself	Deadlines motivate me
Get Involved	Others will…
Modest, Humble	Self Assured
Mature	Less mature
Open Minded	My Opinions
At times moody	Mostly cheerful
Open to change	Not really…
Prefer routine	Adaptable

Transferable Abilities and Skills

The following process will highlight the abilities and skills you enjoy using - and the ones you would like to transfer into your job!

1st) Brainstorm 3-4 experiences that were positive accomplishments.

Ideally you will include job, project or school-related activities so these will be good examples of what you enjoy doing. They do not all need to be recent and can be anything where you feel you succeeded.

Experiences:

#1.______________________________________

#2.______________________________________

#3.______________________________________

#4.______________________________________

2nd) Think through and form a detailed memory of Experience #1. On page 9, write a brief description of that experience. For each experience, focus on what YOU did: Your role, responsibilities, and accomplishments.

3rd) Turn to the "Skills" lists on Pages 11-15.

Thinking through Experience #1, read through the words in the Skills Lists and circle the number (1, 2, 3, 4) if it matches that Experience.

You will most likely start to see a pattern of the types of skills you enjoy using. You can also underline or circle some of these key words to use in your Sales Pitch, Resume, etc.

4th) Repeat this process for Experiences 2-4.

This will provide a detailed picture of the skills you have used and the experience where you used them.

This information is valuable insight and will be used in your resume, sales pitch, interviews and job negotiations.

Experiences
#1)____
____
____
____
____
____

After going through the lists that follow on Pages 11-16, list the primary Skills used in Experience #1:

____
____
____
____
____

#2)____
____
____
____
____
____

After going through the lists that follow on Pages 11-16, list the primary Skills used in Experience #2:

____
____
____
____
____

#3)____

After going through the lists that follow on Pages 11-16, list the primary Skills used in Experience #3:

#4)____

After going through the lists that follow on Pages 11-16, list the primary Skills used in Experience #4:

Circle the number of the Experience that used the Skill, featuring these Mental Processes:

Conceptualizing/Visualizing: imagine; perceive; conceive; pattern recognition; can verbally and mentally paint a picture; three-dimensional/spatial thinking and drawing. #**1** **#2** **#3** **#4**

Evaluating: critical thinking; perceive; assess; edit; discriminate; make decisions; written and verbal comprehension. #**1** **#2** **#3** **#4**

Expediting: action; decisive; anticipate/act. #**1** **#2** **#3** **#4**

Improving: adjust; innovate; improvise; change; new product development; generate new ideas; produce better results; problem solving. #**1** **#2** **#3** **#4**

Initiating/Self-Starting: take action; produce results; motivate; initiate. #**1** **#2** **#3** **#4**

Calculating: pattern recognition; maintain records; calculate; manipulate; records; inventory; bookkeeping; financial accounting. #**1** **#2** **#3** **#4**

Observing: observe; examine; checking; proofreading; seeing differences and similarities; obtaining information; detecting changes. #**1** **#2** **#3** **#4**

Planning/Organizing: developing a plan; strategize; establish goals & objectives; determine priorities; revise; time management; able to delegate; pull it all together. #**1** **#2** **#3** **#4**

Recalling: remembering; memorizing; details of people, events, numbers, music; accurate information retrieval. #**1** **#2** **#3** **#4**

Researching/Analyzing: investigate; analyze; determine; diagnose; study; explore; review; extract; interpret. #**1** **#2** **#3** **#4**

Thinking Creatively: conceive; innovate; invent; develop; design; originality; formulate; devise; produce; synthesize; integrate; solve problems; predict; ideas. #**1** **#2** **#3** **#4**

Circle the number of the Experience that used the Skill, featuring Interpersonal strengths:

Communicating: active listening; speaking or writing clearly; expressing; exchanging; understanding; understanding body language; able to articulate ideas in organized and concise manner. #**1** **#2** **#3** **#4**

Following instructions: understanding requirements and accomplishing; attention to details; follow through; act on instructions to get the job done. #**1** **#2** **#3** **#4**

Leadership of Others or Self: initiate; delegate; self-starter; recognize potential in others; inspire and enlist others; take charge; find skills to complement the group's objectives; motivate. #**1** **#2** **#3** **#4**

Managing/Supervising: communicating goals; directing; motivate; monitor; redirect; encourage; develop; supervise; build a team. #**1** **#2** **#3** **#4**

Negotiate/Deciding: discuss; reconcile; compromise; collaborate; conflict resolution; liaison; listen to different opinions; fairness; diplomatic. #**1** **#2** **#3** **#4**

Persuading: inspire; influence; convince through words and actions; recruit; sell; lead; motivate; negotiate. #**1** **#2** **#3** **#4**

Presenting: confidently addressing small and large groups; public speaking abilities; perform; entertain. #**1** **#2** **#3** **#4**

Interacting with Animals: similar to interacting with people; understanding; feeling; communicating; coaching; leading; taking care of; educating. #**1** **#2** **#3** **#4**

Sensing/Feeling: social perceptiveness; empathy; intuition; responsive; develop rapport; establish connections easily; mediate; warmth. #**1 #2 #3 #4**

Serving: understanding needs of others; customer service; taking care of emotional, physical or medical needs. #**1 #2 #3 #4**

Sharing expertise: knowledgeable; give advice; serve as consultant; guidance. #**1 #2 #3 #4**

Circle the number of the Experience that used the Skill, featuring Hands-on, Physical, & Mechanical Processes:

Documenting/Recording: classify; arrange; make systematic; summarize; transcribing; storing; filing. #**1** **#2** **#3** **#4**

Equipment (Electronic or Mechanical): operating; adjusting; repairing; servicing; calibrate; assemble; maneuver; operate vehicles; piloting; driving. #**1** **#2** **#3** **#4**

Fine motor dexterity: crafts; art; keyboard; musical instruments; keen sense of touch; cooking; tools; precision work. #**1** **#2** **#3** **#4**

Large motor skills: sports; athletic; agile; strength; carrying; loading; balancing. #**1** **#2** **#3** **#4**

Nature: gardening; landscaping; farming: weather and natural elements. #**1** **#2** **#3** **#4**

Technical (Electronic or Mechanical): programming; specialized or routine maintenance; determining tools needed; installing; monitoring; technical design; testing; adapting equipment to user needs; trouble-shooting; quality control; quality assurance. #**1** **#2** **#3** **#4**

ME!

Your Self-Assessment focus has paid off. Review your work up to now and fill in the answers below.

This is an almost effortless way to summarize who you are, your values and skills. This insight will be used in your resume, interviews, Sales Pitch, overview, and networking.

My favorite (transferable) abilities and skills (List 5-8)
Examples: organizing; initiating; managing...

____

____

____

I am... (List 3-6)
Examples: persuasive; happy; a leader; a good delegator; a planner...

____

____

____

I like... (List 3-6)
Examples: researching; communicating; building...

____

____

____

I do not enjoy... (List 3-6)
Examples: Bookkeeping; tedious work; negative people...

____

____

____

I operate best with... (List 3-6)
Examples: some freedom; opportunity to be creative; structure...

____
____
____

Under stress, I... (List 3-6)
Examples: take a deep breath and make a list; go for a run; prioritize...

____
____
____

I am motivated by... (List 3-6)
Examples: positive feedback; success; money; fame; happiness...

____
____
____

[------] would describe me as... (Choose 3 different people; add 3 words for each)
Examples: My boss would describe me as: motivated, organized and creative. My co-worker would describe me as: likeable...

____
____
____
____

For self improvement, I... (List 3-6)
Examples: read; work on my presentation skills; take online courses...

____
____
____

My values include... (List 3-6)
Examples: honesty; integrity; do unto others; stretch oneself...

____

____

____

My short-term goals are... (List 3-6)
Examples: finish my project; find the right job; train for marathon....

____

____

____

Brainstorm: Dream Jobs

This is more than just dreaming, often there are job clues hidden here that you will use to target jobs and industries. Take a minute to think through dream jobs – and why they appeal to you.

Examples:
*Professional Basketball: money; fame; top physical shape.
*International Social Worker: help others; travel; enjoy my job.
*Fashion Designer: creative; cutting edge; wear fun clothes.
*Owner of a Business: be the boss; flexible; status.
*Top Attorney: interesting/stimulating; money; professional.

***List 3-5 jobs. For each job, list 3 reasons why it's attractive to you:**

____
____
____
____
____
____

Brainstorm: People

Focus on the type of people you'd like to be around at work.

Examples:

*Very similar to me: built-in friendships; most comfortable with similar people; shared values.
*Casual: because I'm casual; don't want to work with stiff or stuffy people; I like dressing casual.
*Sports-minded: I like talking sports; a fun environment; helps people build relationships.
*Competitive: I like competing; familiar from sports; best way for me to get ahead.

***Take a minute to think through who you'd like to work with and why. List 3 types of people; give 2 reasons for each:**

____

____

____

Brainstorm: Work Culture

Think through the type of work culture and/or environment you prefer at this point in your life.

Examples:
Professional; Casual/Relaxed; Structured; Creative; Competitive; Serious; Fun; Project-focused; Leave at 5:00pm; Leave when job done; Flexible hours; Fast-paced....

***Select several from the list or add your own:**

____

____

____

____

Brainstorm: Location

Where do you want to live/work? Think through the options.

Examples:
Downtown; Close to home; Big city; Suburbs; Rural;
I'm open– I'll target the best places to find my ideal job.

***Select/add your location preferences and why you find them attractive and/or necessary.**

____
____
____
____
____
____

STEP 2:
All you need to know about Jobs & Industries; Resumes; Your Sales Pitch

Jobs & Industries

You now know a lot about yourself: favorite skills; top interests and values; the types of people, work culture and dream jobs that interest you. Now with Jobs and Industries - -it's a chance to double your job targets! By combining your skills (jobs) and interests (businesses/industries), you will expand your options, stay focused, and discover great career opportunities.

For example:

If you love sports and have an accounting background, you can target sports-related businesses (teams, broadcasting, equipment, marketing firms) for your financial job. Or you could join an accounting firm whose clients include sports teams.

Depending on your interests, you could use your programming skills (skill/job) with an advertising company (creativity) or a software company (technology) or a healthcare provider (health/fitness/helping others).

***Look back to your Dream Jobs. What skills do you want to use?**

List several types of jobs/skills you are interested in:

____
____
____
____
____

Educate yourself on Industries/Businesses.

When you think of a company, think of their businesses, all their businesses….

Examples:

-Coca-Cola: food/beverage, consumer products manufacturing; consumer products sales; marketing, etc.
-Target: retail; online retail; new product development; grocery; merchandising, etc.
-Boeing: aviation; manufacturing; aviation sales; aerospace, etc.
-United Airlines: commercial airline; transportation, customer service, etc.

If you have targeted companies, think through their businesses/industries and list them here:

____

____

____

____

____

Having Trouble?

If you do not know jobs, companies, businesses or industries that you would like to consider, review your information in Step 1. Pay specific attention to Interests, Values, Skills, Dream Jobs and Work Culture. Often it is best to think of a Company or Job that is appealing to you and then work backwards: what are their businesses? What are similar situations?

My Sales Pitch/Elevator Pitch/Overview

This will make your job search and networking so much easier!

Fill in the blanks and answer the questions on the next page to create your own specific, easy to remember descriptor that you can use anywhere! The answers to these questions form an introduction and overview that can be used in casual meetings, networking, and interviews.

-Have I introduced myself?
-Given a quick overview of my skills and/or experience?
-Told what jobs I am interested in?
-Told what industries I am interested in?
-What's my follow-up line?

Examples:
"Hello, I am a recent college graduate with strong leadership, teamwork and research experience. I am most interested in communications, customer service or entry-level marketing positions in advertising firms or non-profits. Some of the companies I'm targeting include CCC, XYZ and 123 Corp. May I call you to get your thoughts and ideas over a quick cup of coffee?"

"Hello, I am currently starting a job search and have strong experience in accounting and supervisory roles. I'm most interested in accounts payable, receivables or collections management jobs in the manufacturing or technology industries. Some of the companies I'm targeting include CCC, XYZ and 123 Corp. May I stop by your office for 5 or 10 minutes to drop off my resume and get your thoughts and ideas?"

Fill in your Sales Pitch below:

Hello, I am ______________________________with
____and
_____________________________.

I am most interested in _______________, or jobs in either the _________________, or _______________ industries.

Some of the companies I am targeting include _________________, _________________, or
____.

I'd love to (get your thoughts) (tell you a little more about myself) (send you my resume)
____
____.

Say it out loud and rewrite it until it flows naturally:

____
____
____
____
____

Resumes and Cover Letters

Resume Tips

*Present your information clearly and always honestly.

*Use keywords that relate to the jobs you've done and the jobs you are targeting.

*Think about what you have actually done in your jobs and list these accomplishments.

*Proofread backwards and have a friend review to ensure everything is correct.

*Do not use "Objective" – instead, think about an "Overview" using bullet points or descriptive sentences to make it easy to understand your experience. (Look at your Sales Pitch.)

*List your Education below your Experience, unless you are a very recent graduate.

*Do not list References or state that they are available. It's understood that they will ask for them.

*Highlight your accomplishments and achievements with specifics: numbers, percentages, rankings, reporting relationships, etc.

*If you use a nickname or have an androgynous name, you may include the nickname or Mr./Ms. to help the reader: (Ms.) Terry Patrick Walton.

*Do not use: I, my, his, her, etc. This is a document about you, so you do not need to add these.

*Turn the final resume into a PDF or protected document. Use "Your Name Resume.pdf" to make it easy to find.

*Remember: "You" Are Your Resume: Be sure your voicemail, email address, social media, etc. are all professional.

Your Resume

Use "Overview" at the beginning, selecting strong descriptors in bullet point form, or 1-2 strong sentences. (See your Sales Pitch for ideas.)

Fill in your "Experience" adding words, phrases and ideas from the Transferable Abilities and Skills on pages 11-15.

Move "Education" to the end of the resume. Incorporate the Resume Tips listed on the preceding pages.

It is appropriate to leave your address off, including only your email and phone.

After you complete your resume and Sales Pitch, you will then work on your cover letter.

Templates

We recommend using traditional (free) templates, either on Word, Google Doc, etc.

Recent Grad Name Here

1670 address here
Your City, ST zip

Cell: (555) 555-5555
YOURS@email.com

Overview

Recent Business graduate with logistics, commodities and consumer industry experience. Strengths in communication, problem solving, customer relations, evaluation/analytics and business solutions.

Education

YOUR College

Bachelor of Science in Business **2014**

Courses: Managerial Accounting, Global Operations and Technology, International Management, International Marketing, International Financial Management, Global Strategic Management

Minor: Spanish

Experience

XYZ COMPANY HERE

Assistant to Accounting Manager, *Tampa, FL* **Summer 2013**

- Responsible for accurate accounting and recording of Company transactions.
- Balanced journal entries for the Credit department on daily basis.
- Updated insurance files; Communicated across departments.
- Accurately adjusted millions of dollars in Company transactions.
- Reported to the Accounting Manager.

EDF COMPANY HERE

Assistant in Transportation, *Tampa, FL* **Summer 2011**

- Responsible for project management of CRM update program.
- Updated thousands of contacts in Company CRM files to help improve logistics efficiency.
- Communication with Customers and Company transportation, technical and sales departments.
- Daily phone, data and online research to insure accurate files.
- Utilized communication skills and creative problem solving to develop relationships.
- Reported to the Transportation Manager.

Other

Summer jobs:

AAA Café - 2012
MMM Landscaping - 2012
12345 Landscaping - 2010
BEST Day Camp - 2008

Volunteer:

Habitat for Humanity Store - 2013
Homeless Shelter - San Jose, Costa Rica -2013
Reviving Baseball in the Inner City - 2010

Study Abroad

Costa Rica, Summer 2013

Your Name

5555 address, City, St Zip

C 555-555-5555 • YOURemail@email.com

Sales, management and financial professional with strong analytical, relationship development, communication and project management skills. Experience in sales, team and relationship management, financial analysis, and small business operations in financial, sales, marketing, and service industries.

EXPERIENCE

XYZ BANK, ST Petersburg, FL **Mortgage Loan Officer** **June 2012 – Present**

- Originate an average of $XXX million in new mortgage origination and sales each month through proactive analysis, sales, marketing and relationships.
- Analyze Clients' current debt and devise proactive solutions in refinancing and debt consolidation with Bank's products.
- Client sales and management involves:
    - Relationship development and Sales
    - Analytical and critical thinking
    - Problem solving and resolution
    - Clear communication of complex refinancing options
    - Coordination with internal and external partners
    - Project management/follow through to complete transactions.
- Product knowledge includes: conventional and government backed loans
- High borrower retention and customer satisfaction through specifically tailored debt consolidation.
- On-going training and education in finance, banking, legal changes, sales, marketing, and new products.

ABC Financial Group, Houston, TX **Unit Sales Manager** **2010 – 2011**

- Sales Manager selected for team of managers to establish Company's first mortgage center in Texas.
- Managed and trained a team of Loan officers in financing, sales, and time management.
- Maintained one of the highest customer retention and loan closing rates in company.
- Cornerstone Sales Award Winner

12345 Media Company LLC, Orlando, FL **Account Management, Finance & Operations** **2009-2010**

- Launched and operated start-up with cutting edge proprietary marketing for digital signage.
- Negotiated joint venture with NNN Media, launching various marketing platforms in Central FL.
- Researched and analyzed demographic study to summarize the company's target market.
- Creatively directed clients in establishing marketing plans and budgets.
- Execution of Clients' marketing plans through internet, digital, television, and print media.

UNIVERSITY Department of Engineering **Product Development Intern** **2009**

- Developed product ideas and marketing schemes for Ultra Compact Electromagnetic Generators.
- Formulated a business plan and model for selected products to be powered by micro-scale generators.
- Business plan competed in Global Venture Challenge.

EDUCATION

Your University Here - Graduate School of Business **CITY, STATE**
M.A. International Business **2009**
Courses: International Trade, Globalization & Business, Global Strategic Management, Logistics, International Finance
Certificates: Global Business; New Venture Creations
Thesis: XXX's Strategic Management Monopoly

Your University Here – College of Business Administration **CITY, STATE**
B.A. Business Administration **2008**
Courses: Finance, Economics, Managerial Accounting, Commodities, Principles of Management, Managerial Economics, Future Markets and Risk, Business Finance
Minors: Entrepreneurship; Management

OTHER

Your Club/Fraternity/Association- Alumni President; Leadership positions 2006-2009
ANY EARLIER WORK THAT MAY BE INTERESTING/RELEVANT
ANY HONORS YOU HAVE HERE AAA Business Honor Society
VOLUNTEER WORK/INTERESTS HERE

Cover Letters

Choose one of the recommended traditional letter templates in Google docs, Word, etc.

Use your information from the ME! Section on pages 16-18, key adjectives, descriptions and experience from your Resume, key traits from your Sales Pitch, and your targeted job/industry.

Insert this information appropriately into each cover letter, tailoring it to fit the job/person/company/opportunity. You will have 3-4 clear and concise paragraphs.

1st: Start with an introductory sentence or two. If someone has referred you, mention his or her name now.

2nd paragraph is about how your school/work experience is relevant to the company and the job. Show that you have done your research on the company.

3rd paragraph is more detail on how you and your experience are a good fit for the company and the job.

Closing: Restate your interest; thank them for their time; state your follow-up action. "I appreciate the opportunity to apply for the Accounting Manager position with CCC Corp. I am very interested in joining your team and will follow up next week."

The following examples represent concise, to the point cover letters:

222 W. Franklin Street
Oakland, CA XXXXX
November 10, 20XX

Mr. Frank Jones
Manager-Accounting
ABC Corporation
555 E 5th Street
San Francisco, CA XXXXX

Dear Mr. Jones:

Robert Smith encouraged me to contact you. My resume is attached; I am considering a career move and have a strong interest in joining ABC Corporation.

I have admired ABC for years and know it to be an innovative and progressive culture. I am currently an Associate Manager of Payroll at 123 Inc. and am responsible for a team of 5. I have strong people, project, and time management skills, a detail-orientation, and enjoy working in a fast-paced environment. My writing and communication skills have enabled me to add responsibilities at 123 and I would look forward to being a contributing member of your team.

Thank you for your time and the opportunity to share my resume and interest with you. I will follow up next week.

Sincerely,

James Harris

P.O. Box 0000
Franklin, IL XXXXX
October 19, 20XX

Ms. Jane Doe
Human Resources Manager
ABC Consulting
888 Oak Street
Des Moines, IA XXXXX

Dear Ms. Doe:
I spoke with John Smith at the recent Career Fair and he suggested I contact you. This letter and the attached resume serve as my application for the Associate position at ABC Consulting. I believe my skills, academic training, and work experience are a strong fit for this position.

I graduate with a Business degree from U of C in spring 20XX. I have developed strong analytical and communication skills through my courses and team projects. In addition, my hands-on experience and student leadership positions contribute to my qualifications.

As an intern at CCC Corporation this past summer, I focused on client engagement, data retrieval, and internal communications. My previous experience includes customer sales and service in the retail industry, and developing survey materials for a national consulting company. On campus, I have demonstrated leadership ability by serving in elected volunteer roles, and organizing community events. These involvements allowed me to plan and organize my time, work well on teams, and further develop interpersonal, oral, and written communications skills.

Thank you for your time and the opportunity to present my background. I am interested in the Associate position and will follow up next week.

Sincerely,
Kathy Jones

STEP 3: Interviews

Interviewing is a skill; You can be a Pro.

To improve any skill you need 2 things: knowledge and practice. Throughout Pages 36-80, we uncover the key Insiders' Knowledge on:

-Top Tips for Interviews
-Types of Interviews and What to Do
-The Different Interviewing Styles
-Tips for Introverts and Extroverts
-THE Interview Strategies and Answers

Tips and Rules for Interviews

1. Arrive 10 minutes early.

2. Bring a copy of your resume. Do not assume the interviewer has read it.

3. Be nice and likable; people want to work with people they like. Treat everyone in the building as someone who can say "yes" or "no" to hiring you.

4. Turn off your cell phone! And do NOT look at it for ANY reason. Wear a watch.

5. If asked if you'd like coffee, etc., keep it simple: water only!

6. Use your manners! Please, thank you, don't talk with your mouth full...

7. Do not use "meal" interviews as a chance to pig-out. Eat a snack before, order an easy-to-eat option (you will be doing most of the talking), and treat the waitress, busboy, etc with respect. If your interviewer/host orders an alcoholic drink, you may also - but only one. This is an interview; stay focused.

8. Be confident: 1) Handshake: firm grip with good eye contact. Shake females' hands the same way - no wimpy grips. Practice on a friend. 2) Posture: standing & sitting- straight back, relaxed shoulders. 3) Smile: it makes everything better.

9. Develop and maintain a conversational rapport in the interview: good standing and sitting posture, eye contact, smiles, active listening, and relaxed body language.

10. Prepare several small talk "starters" - sports, weather, artwork, photos. Never talk about anything negative ("traffic was terrible!") and never religion or politics. If the interviewer brings these up, respond with a polite, non-judgmental answer.

11. Not too much... wear simple jewelry; light cologne; medium heels; modest, professional attire; no loud ties or too short skirts. Hair: neat and out of the way. Most often, clean-shaven is best.

12. Have 1 or 2 interview outfits/suits that are foolproof: wrinkle-free, fast & easy, business-like and comfortable. Dress for the job you want, not your current situation.

13. Develop several lines to give you extra time as you think of answers. "Let me think for a minute", "Oh, that's an interesting question", "I have several examples, let me think which one might be most interesting to you."

14. If the interviewer is interrupted with a phone call, stay professional and patient; you are still in the interview. If a company co-worker interrupts the interview, be prepared to stand up, introduce yourself and make a good impression. Now 2 people are impressed with you!

15. If you can, do not talk "money"- save that for later in the interview process.

Types of Interviews

Informational Interview

This is a meeting to learn about someone's job, career path or industry.

Networking Interview

This is similar to informational, but a little more casual. You may have set it up through a mutual contact. Your goal: impress them and add more contacts for networking.

For both of these, you need to:

-Do background research on the person, job, company and industry so you can develop good questions to ask.

-Bring a copy of your resume.

-Be prepared to tell them about You. Be ready to sell yourself!

-Be considerate of their time. Keep it to 20-30 minutes and they will look forward to seeing you again.

-Politely ask if they can think of others for you to meet.

-Follow up with a Thank You email or note; add them to your active Networking List.

One on One Interview

This is a real interview focused on a specific job.

You need to:

-Do job and company research; try to find out about the Interviewer.

-Bring a copy of your resume.

-Prepare your key points: how your background, experience, and accomplishments make you the best candidate.

-Anticipate their questions and concerns; look for opportunities to talk about your key points.

-Have several thoughtful questions prepared for them.

-Ask them for their business card; ask if you may follow up if you have other questions.

-Follow up with a Thank You email/note; add them to your active Networking List.

Group Interview

The company brings in a group of candidates to interview at the same time.

You need to:

-Do job and company research, try to find out about the Interviewer.

-Bring a copy of your resume.

-Be polite and nice to your "competition" and initiate small talk.

-Prepare your key points: how your background, experience, and accomplishments make you the best candidate.

-Anticipate their questions and concerns; look for opportunities to talk about your key points.

-Have several thoughtful questions prepared for them.

-Feel comfortable promoting yourself with your "competition" in the room.

-Shake hands with the Interviewer(s) and thank them as you leave.

-Ask them for their business card; ask if you may follow up if you have other questions.

-Follow up with a Thank You email/note; add them to your active Networking List.

Panel Interview

This is you against the world.... just kidding, but it may feel like it! Several people will interview you, and one or all may ask questions.

You need to:

-Do job and company research; try to find out about members of the panel.

-Bring multiple copies of your resume.

-Develop some "rapport" with each of them: Make initial eye contact with the one who asked the question, then proceed to look at the others as you answer.

-Prepare your key points: how your background, experience, and accomplishments make you the best candidate.

-Anticipate their questions and concerns; look for opportunities to talk about your key points.

-Have several thoughtful questions prepared for them.

-Ask each for their business cards; ask if you may follow up if you have other questions.

-Shake hands with each person and thank them as you leave.

-Follow up with a Thank You email/note to each; add them to your active Networking List.

Video Interview

This can be over the computer, phone or at a video conferencing center.

You will need to:

-Do job and company research; try to find out about the Interviewer.

-If you are at home, be sure your video "background" is clean and professional.

-Wear solids, nothing patterned that may be distracting.

-Sit at a desk/table with water, resume, papers and pens. Phone, TV, music: OFF. No animals or distractions.

-Be sure your video camera is level with your face.

-Relax, smile and build rapport.

-Be sure the Interviewer has a copy of your resume.

-Prepare your key points: how your background, experience, and accomplishments make you the best candidate.

-Anticipate their questions and concerns; look for opportunities to talk about your key points.

-Have several thoughtful questions prepared for them.

-Ask if you may follow up if you have other questions.

-Follow up with a Thank You email/note; add them to your active Networking List.

Phone Interview

Ace this to get a face-to-face interview; do not miss this chance!

It should be scheduled; do not agree to a "have I caught you at a good time?" interview. If you are not ready, politely ask if you can call back in 5 minutes, an hour, a day: it is most important for you to be focused and ready. Have a professional voicemail message.

You need to:

-Be sure you have strong, clear cell coverage or a landline.

-Understand clearly the timing and who will initiate the call.

-Get dressed; brush your teeth. Smile, relax and build rapport.

-Sit at a desk/table with water, resume, papers and pens. Phone, TV, music: OFF. No animals or distractions.

-Do not use your speakerphone, even if they are.

-Be sure the Interviewer has a copy of your resume.

-Prepare your key points: how your background, experience, and accomplishments make you the best candidate.

-Anticipate their questions/concerns; get your key points across.

-Have several thoughtful questions prepared for them. Ask if you may follow up if you have other questions.

-Follow up with a Thank You email/note; add them to your active Networking List.

*Beware...
Different Types of Interviewers

The Hijacker
This interviewer takes over and changes the subject to whatever he/she is interested in. You need to politely figure out how to get the focus back on your skills and accomplishments. "...I agree, and that's why I'm so interested in working at..." "That reminds me of a challenge I faced last year...".

The Big Talker
This interviewer does all the talking. He/she will think it was a great meeting – but know nothing about you. Again, you need to politely figure out how to get the focus back on your skills and accomplishments. "...that's so interesting, I'm not sure even my strong persuasive skills could have helped me there...", "That sounds like a great vacation; hopefully one day I can also do that, but right now I am so interested in this position ...".

The "I Don't Know Why I Am Interviewing You"
Do not get flustered. Calmly go into your overview/sales pitch and then reference the actual position. If you have the chance, continue by telling how your experience makes you the best candidate for the job.

The Inexperienced
This interviewer will need your help. Spoon feed them with your accomplishments and work highlights; help them make small talk; and keep the interview focused.

The Late/Busy/Fast
Do not get flustered. Be gracious, understanding and appreciative of their time – they will remember you fondly for helping them out!

The "I Haven't Seen Your Resume"
Do not get flustered; provide him/her with a copy and a minute to look it over.

The Cancellation
Do not show frustration. Be gracious, understanding and accommodating. Politely ask about rescheduling and how to follow up. They will feel guilty, so definitely reschedule!

The "Do you know?"
This interviewer only wants to talk about people, places and things that you have in common. You need to politely figure out how to get the focus back on your skills and accomplishments. "...I do know him, actually he has given me several networking contacts in my job search..." "She's great; her former professor is one of my references ..".

The Bad Cop
This interviewer wants to scare you into revealing everything. Relax, take a deep breath, think through your answers and try to build rapport.

The Best Friend
This interviewer wants you to feel so comfortable that you share all of your secrets. Don't! Remember –this is an interview. Do not talk about how much you hate early mornings, travel, hangovers.... Be professional at all times.

Tips for Introverts and Extroverts

If you are more Introverted:

-You think before you speak – that's good!

-You are less likely to run on and on with your answers.

-Try email and phone (with a script) as a way to get comfortable with networking.

-You will do well in one on one meetings; quick coffee, etc.

-In all meetings, be prepared to make small talk to help establish rapport.

-Smile so you relax.

-Send thoughtful follow-ups to your contacts.

-Don't let yourself get too deep in research; be sure to set up meetings, preferably one a day to keep you connected.

If you are more Extroverted:

-You establish rapport easily – that's good!

-Try to set up daily meetings to keep yourself energized.

-Watch yourself in meetings: stop talking after a couple of sentences; don't run on and on - you will get yourself in trouble.

-Don't get too friendly too fast; stay professional in all meetings.

-Take a deep breath to slow yourself down; let silent pauses happen.

-You naturally think out loud while talking – stop! Take a minute to think before you speak. Stay focused and specific.

Interviews - Questions & Answers

Here it is!

All the Interview Q & A Strategies* to answer questions, make conversation and represent yourself honestly and favorably.

Read through the strategies and sample answers; make notes on your own answers, and practice. Take the time to answer the questions out loud – to yourself or a friend- - so you are accustomed to hearing yourself. ...And it's even easier the 2nd and 3rd time you practice.

***Now that you know your skills, values, interests, experiences, and targets you can apply these interview strategies to most all interview questions.**

1. Tell me about yourself.

STRATEGY

This is an easy question for them to ask - and it's a great opportunity to get across the important information you want to share: your current situation, your background and skills, your strengths, and your accomplishments.

You developed this "Sales Pitch/Elevator Pitch" on page 27 and you will use it here. Do not talk about where you are from, your family, etc. Be sure to end strong, because chances are, the next question will start there.

EXAMPLES

Networking Meeting: "Well, I am a recent graduate, with strong research and analytical skills. I majored in business, knowing that would work well with my sales and leadership experience. I am interested in sales, marketing or research opportunities in the consumer products and financial services industries."

Specific Interview: "I recently graduated with a degree in business. I have strong skills in research and analysis, and have experience in sales and leadership through my retail jobs and involvement in community service organizations. I have always respected your company and am very interested in your sales training program."

"I am currently Manager of Accounts Payable at CCC Corp and manage a team of 4 people. I have experience in several industries…."

2. What did you study in school? Why? Will it be useful in your career?

STRATEGY
It doesn't matter if you studied journalism rather than economics, at this point you want to talk about how you really enjoyed it and what skills you learned: research; writing; presentation; critical analysis; teamwork; debate; conceptual; etc.

Take the time to think through how you benefitted and link that to how you will use it in life and/or work.

EXAMPLE
"I actually was an Art History major, which may seem strange since I am applying for a communications position. But interestingly, I really learned how to research, write, present and defend positions. I feel my oral and written communication skills are stronger, and they will help me in my career and life."

My interview strategy notes:

____

____

____

____

____

____

____

3. What do you do for self-improvement/professional development?

STRATEGY

This is an opportunity to show you are always trying to get better- -not that you are trying to "fix" a problem. Want a stronger understanding of a different part of the business? Interested in getting an industry-related license? Have you always wanted to learn another language or read more? Training for a marathon? Interested in the stock market? Golf? Community Service? Taking an art, finance, cooking, public speaking, or web design class at the local community college?

All of these can become good answers - just be sure it is something you really have considered/are doing.

EXAMPLES

"Even though I'm in the human resources department, I am taking an on-line course in accounting so I can better understand my internal clients. I also love to play golf, which everyone knows requires on-going self-improvement!"

"I've been training for a marathon. Not only do I love the exercise, but I find it is a great time for me to think and unwind from a stressful day. Professionally, I am interested in getting my CFA and have looked into taking a class."

"I am a volunteer and have had to make several Board presentations. This has been a great way for me to work on my public speaking and networking skills. I also love to read, so I download books and listen while I drive."

4. Why do you want this job?

STRATEGY
Be sure you have thought this through before the interview and lined up the job's responsibilities with your skills. You will want to be specific and pull in how your background and accomplishments make you the best candidate. You need to let them know how interested you are!

Break it into: the company; the position; your background.

EXAMPLES
"First of all, I have always admired CCC Inc. Secondly, the market research position is one where I can use my business and interpersonal skills to excel. My internship gave me an overview of your industry and I gained strong analytical experience. I have enjoyed meeting the people in the department and feel certain I can soon be a contributing member of the team."

"I have always viewed CCC as the industry leader. So the opportunity to join as an Account Executive is one that I am very interested in. My sales experience in professional services and medical products will be invaluable to me as I take on new and existing customers. I put a lot of energy into relationships, both internal and external, and know that at CCC, this will continue to be an area where I get a lot of career satisfaction."

5. What has been your favorite job? What is your dream job?

STRATEGY

The interviewer wants to find out what you like to do - and what you don't like to do. Think through the best parts of your current or most recent job and highlight the ones that line up with what you are looking for.

It is always best if you can say your current job is your favorite - no one wants to hire someone who isn't currently happy. For your dream job, think of one that would allow you to talk about all the skills you love - and that this position needs.

EXAMPLES

"Favorite job? Hmmm, it probably is my current role. I really enjoy the people I work with, and the projects I've been working on lately have been challenging, interesting and rewarding. I really enjoy knowing that the recommendations I've made have been put into action."

"Dream job? Let me think.... I think if I were given the chance, I'd love to be the top engineer on a major bridge project. In my current role, I have complete responsibility, on a much smaller scale, so I think I'd like to take that to the extreme with say, the next Golden Gate Bridge."

6. Why are you leaving? Why did you leave?

STRATEGY

Your answer needs to be all about the future and where you want to go. Nothing negative about the past.

Determine the best parts of the new position (not the money; not less travel; not easier commute...) and play those up. Industry leader; more responsibility; opportunity to expand on your knowledge; return to managing and growing people; etc.

EXAMPLES

"Actually, I am still very happy and challenged in my current role, but thought this looked interesting. I hoped we could talk further; you can learn more about my background and I can learn more about this opportunity."

"Actually, when I came across this opportunity, I was surprised by how well it lines up with my skills, and so I looked a little deeper. That's when I first spoke with the recruiter and learned about the exciting plans for this department."

"I actually left my position 6 weeks ago. As much as I enjoyed CCC Inc. our department has been cut dramatically. I still have great respect for the team there and lots of good friends in the company. And that's what I thought was interesting about this opportunity, the product/culture/values/customers/etc. are similar and play to my strengths."

7. What's been your worst job? Worst boss?

STRATEGY

You know the answer here - you've never had a worst job or bad boss! That's right, once again, you will find the positives in everything. And if you are backed in a corner and have to say something, reach back really far and make it benign.

EXAMPLES

"Worst job? Oh, let me think. Well, I'm not sure I've had a worst job; I feel like I've enjoyed most all of my jobs, and have certainly learned and grown from them."

"Ok, well if I had to come up with something, I guess it would be "worst part of a job." When I worked at Starbucks, we sometimes had to clean up the cigarette butts from the mulched areas outside. They were soggy and smelly, so it certainly was my least favorite part of what, overall, was a fun job."

"Worst boss?" That's a tough one. I don't think I've had a bad boss. I guess I've been lucky that way."

My interview strategy notes:

____

____

____

____

____

____

8. How would your boss/professor/co-worker/team describe you?

STRATEGY

Brilliantly, the introduction of a 3rd party, even in name only, makes us think twice about what the Boss, etc. would say. So think it through now, with the focus on your positive traits. And be prepared, they may ask if you would you agree with the description.

EXAMPLES

"Oh, that's an interesting thought. I think my boss would describe me as productive, efficient and organized."

"I think my co-workers would say I am always ready to pitch in, like to complete projects and fun to work with."

9. Tell me about your strengths and weaknesses.

STRATEGY
You will have thought this through and will be ready. What you need to talk about is a weakness that is small, or that might apply to you "outside" of the job, and that you have worked on.

Another option is to mention something that would not be important in your job (an accountant saying he is not creative; an artist saying they are not good at balancing their checkbook). Start with this and then quickly go into your strengths.

EXAMPLES
"Oh, for weakness, I always have wanted to be better at public speaking. I've read a book on tips and asked my current boss for more opportunities to present to upper management. As for my strengths, I am an accomplished and creative graphic artist who understands client timeframes."

"I'm really not as good about planning my free time as I'd like to be. I am so structured during the workweek, that sometimes I find I haven't planned anything for the weekend. My strengths include a strong financial background and very good client relationship skills."

"Sometimes I try to squeeze in everything on the weekend and plan too much to do. As for my strengths, I am a strong communicator with a strategic marketing mind. "

"I am not as knowledgeable about international business as I'd like, so I've made a point to read international news websites on a regular basis. As for my strengths, I feel I am detail-oriented, business-minded and customer focused."

10. Tell me about a problem/issue/challenge you've faced.

STRATEGY

Again, you will be prepared for this one. You will want to talk about something that happened a while back. Take a minute to think through how you will answer and be sure to end on an upbeat, positive note.

EXAMPLES

"When I first joined CCC, I didn't realize the importance of keeping my boss's peers informed. But at CCC, all of the managers take an interest in you and want to be involved in your professional development. My boss gave me the feedback early on, so I was able to give casual updates in the elevator, lunchroom, etc. It really turned out well; I developed some great relationships and definitely grew professionally."

"My former boss was not the most natural communicator and this made it difficult for me to gauge how I was doing. A friend recommended I talk with him and this made a big difference. At times, I still needed to initiate the conversation, but I realized that it made us both more successful."

11. Are you happy in your current role?

STRATEGY

YES! No one wants to hire someone who is not happy; they view past performance as an indicator of future performance. So think through what you like about your job and your reasons for looking (review questions 4 and 6). Keep it positive.

EXAMPLES

"I have been happy. I really like my co-workers and our product."

"Yes, CCC is a great company."

"Yes, my manager is very creative."

12. What motivates you?

STRATEGY

Aren't you glad you thought these things through? Be honest here and think how it ties to your job/interview. Most answers are acceptable; but "more free time" and "being able to sleep late" are not.

EXAMPLES

"I am motivated by several things: adding value; doing what's right and working smart."

"Ok, I'll admit it. I am motivated by money and that's why I enjoy sales. Of course, I also am motivated by doing a good job, intellectual challenges, and having good relationships."

"I am motivated by being the best I can be, contributing to others, and feeling that what I do makes a difference."

My interview strategy notes:

____

____

____

____

____

____

13. What are you proudest of?

STRATEGY

Personally or professionally proud, or both. Be honest, use a recent example and think of how it relates to you and your job search. Show enthusiasm!

EXAMPLES

"Well, personally I am most proud of having completed the local Triathlon last year. Professionally, I think a recent project we finished was just fantastic; the client loved it and our whole team felt great!"

"A recent accomplishment that I am very proud of is the hiring of a new client services team. We had some very specific needs and we were able to bring in the right mix of people."

"Having recently graduated, I am proud of a senior research assignment I completed. I also am very proud that I excelled at my summer job as a waitress. It took a lot of energy, patience, and skill. Actually, that job is what made me realize I thrive in busy environments."

14. What disappointments have you had in your job/life/school? What would you do differently?

STRATEGY

Thoughtful, reflective answers will win you points. But do not go to extremes! Keep your disappointments distant, and be sure you have learned from them.

EXAMPLES

"When I was applying for college, I really wanted to go to ____ . I was deferred but was accepted to my 2nd choice. Initially I was disappointed, but I decided to go to ______ and have never regretted it!"

"When I joined CCC I had an entry level position in Human Resources but my dream job was in finance. So, I really wanted to move into financial analysis... until I tried Compensation and Benefits. I had no idea how much my skills lined up with this field. So I'm glad my disappointment led me to a career I love."

"I thought I wanted to play college sports but was sidelined with an injury my junior year in high school. I was so mad at first, but it gave me a chance to step back and really analyze where I wanted to spend my time. I continued to play sports in high school, but turned my focus to my studies and community service, so no, I would not do it differently."

15. Are you the best performer in your department? Group? Team? Class?

STRATEGY

Be careful here; these are the "either-or" questions that you need to answer thoughtfully.

Either you are the best performer and are a self-consumed jerk OR you are not a strong member of the team and probably not a good hire. You must recognize others' contributions, share the credit, and make your own contributions stand out.

EXAMPLES

"Oh, that's a tricky question. I'd say we all are good performers. My strengths are in project management, communications and details, and these complement my co-workers' strengths."

"Our team is organized to take advantage of our different strengths: Jim is good at creative concepts; Jane is a skilled writer; Holly is great at client management; and I am very organized and strategic. It really makes it a productive, enjoyable environment."

16. Where do you want to be in 3-5 years?

STRATEGY

There is a balance needed: ambition vs. patience; focused vs. flexible; specific vs. general. You will need to think about the company and job you are interviewing for, their culture, and the opportunities to move up.

EXAMPLES

"Well, I love sales so I can see myself still being in sales but having a bigger territory. I could also move into sales management, but I would not want to give up an active sales role."

"I love graphic design, so I know I'd still be designing. I'd like more complex projects, some client interaction, and possibly some training responsibilities."

"I am interested in marketing as my career. So while I am starting in marketing communications, I'd like to gain experience in marketing research and strategy. I'd like to be in a junior management position in 5 years."

17. Tell me about your current responsibilities and accomplishments.

STRATEGY

For this answer, clearly cite your responsibilities and your reporting relationships, and then focus on your accomplishments. Be concise and interesting; watch their body language cues to see if you are talking too long or losing them.

EXAMPLES

"I am currently responsible for recruiting for the technology division. I manage 2 recruiters and report to the VP. Our recent accomplishments include...."

"I work in the communications department and report to the Director of Public Relations. I am responsible for weekly employee and customer emails, social media strategy and updates, assisting on the annual report, general proofing and editing duties. My latest accomplishments have been...."

"Currently, I am a substitute teacher while I look for a technology job. I also volunteer at an afterschool program where I am teaching a website design class. This has been a great way for me to stay current and feel I am accomplishing something worthwhile."

18. What traits do you admire in others? What people/companies do you admire?

STRATEGY

Through your research on yourself, the company and the job, you know your values and the company's. After the question is asked, take a minute so you can pull these together for a thoughtful answer.

EXAMPLES

"I value integrity and perseverance in others and myself. That's one reason I admire my former boss so much. He taught me..."

"My English professor (my mom, my uncle...) always valued creativity, but not without usefulness. So I think that rubbed off on me. And I think that's one reason I admire Apple so much."

My interview strategy notes:

____

____

____

____

____

____

____

19. What in your experience makes you right for this job?

STRATEGY

You have already thought about the skills this job will need and through your own skills. You are ready to line it up beautifully for them - they'll love it!

EXAMPLES

"My experience as a waitress prepared me for the fast action, customer service and multi-tasking that this job requires. Also, as a Tutor in college, I had to quickly come up to speed on a variety of subjects so I know I'll be able to do that here."

"I know that in this job I will need strong management and communication skills. As an Assistant Retail Manager, I dealt with many personnel, customer and corporate issues, which prepared me well."

20. If you could.... have dinner with anyone? Change the world? Be an animal?

STRATEGY

Your answer here doesn't matter as much as the reasoning behind your answer. Often it is best to start out with "well, if I had longer to think about it..." and then give your answer and your reasons. Read the news so you can be up to date on current events, sports and news. These are usually good options.

EXAMPLES

"Well if I had longer to think about it, I might come up with something else, but I guess I'd like to have dinner with _______ to get the real inside scoop on why he felt he needed steroids."

"If I had longer.... I recently read an article on the drought and starvation in...."

"...My great grandfather was killed in World War I and I would love a chance to meet him...."

21. Who are you most like in your family/office/friends and why?

STRATEGY

On this type of question, think through it before you start answering. Get rid of any "family/school jokes" and be careful and thoughtful. When you are asked about your friends, think of your most impressive friend; people are often similar to those their friends.

EXAMPLES

"I think I am most like my dad because we both are math-oriented; but then again, my sister and I both like being outdoors and entertaining friends."

"In my office, most of us are very conscientious. My boss has a high energy level and so do I; we also have a similar communication style. So I guess, my boss."

"My friends are mostly focused and dedicated; in fact, we have a hard time seeing each other except on the weekends. We do seem to share the same values and interests, though."

22. What have you been told to work on in performance reviews?

STRATEGY

Think through your projects and jobs and be ready for this. You will want to use a distant comment, and one that you have improved.

EXAMPLES

"I've had 2 very different retail experiences. In my first, there was a "do not sell/push" philosophy. In my 2nd, there was an "approach the customer and sell" philosophy. So in my first week on the 2nd job, my manager talked to me. It took some effort, but my co-workers were really great about giving me tips and informal training on their assertive sales philosophy."

"Early on, I was not a naturally organized person. Luckily for me, my boss had a great system and I learned from her. I saw what a difference it made and eagerly adapted it to my style."

My interview strategy notes:

____

____

____

____

____

____

23. What is the difference between a manager and a leader?

STRATEGY

Think through managers and leaders you've seen throughout your life. A manager may be that because of title; a leader often doesn't have the title. Use personal examples if you have them.

EXAMPLES

"The best manager I had was a natural leader. She was skilled in the "management" side, but also knew how to get us on board. So to me, the difference is between title and natural abilities."

"I think a manager is more someone who has the job, but maybe not the vision. A real leader has the vision, and the abilities to get people to share that vision."

24. How did you hear about this job?

STRATEGY

This is an opportunity to show that you are focused and targeted in your job search. If you heard about it from a "friend" make it sound more intentional; if you came across it on a job website, mention that you had targeted this company or type of job.

EXAMPLES

"One of my contacts knew I was targeting CCC and passed along the job lead."

"I have targeted several companies, CCC being at the top of the list, and I regularly go on your website to see what opportunities might be available."

"I was contacted by a recruiter who told me about the opportunity. It really caught my attention; CCC is such an impressive company and this sounds like a position where I could thrive."

25. What's more important, interpersonal skills or job skills?

STRATEGY

This is another one of the either-or questions where you can't win if you trap yourself in a box - you need to speak to both sides. You will want to highlight the advantages of both.

EXAMPLES

"That's a tough one. For most jobs, I really see the value in both. You need to have interpersonal skills to work within and across an organization, but you must have the actual job skills to get the job done and have credibility."

"I think most all jobs need both. In my sales job, I certainly need the interpersonal skills to establish the relationships, but if I didn't have the technical skills, I couldn't close the deal."

26. What job/people do you find difficult and why?

STRATEGY

Remember to stay positive; your comments reflect on you. Think of things that are benign, or are not related to your job.

EXAMPLES

"I can't think of any "people" I find difficult. As for jobs, sometimes it's difficult to focus on the after-project "cleanup" details; there really aren't any parts of my job that I dislike, but I do enjoy some parts more than others."

"Difficult people? I'm not really sure about that; I guess that might be more situational. Difficult jobs? This really isn't a "work" job, but I'm not wild about filling out insurance forms, etc."

27. How do you motivate others?

STRATEGY

Think through how you like to be motivated and what you can pull from that: listening; communication; positive reinforcement; clear goals; etc.

EXAMPLES

"I feel all people are different and you need to figure out what motivates them. That's why I believe in lots of open communication early on, so you can set goals together."

"I try to understand my team so I know what works best for each. It may be a little different for each, but positive reinforcement is usually a part of it."

My interview strategy notes:

____

____

____

____

____

____

28. What do you do for fun? What's a perfect day for you?

STRATEGY

Think about what you like to do - but do not say: "just hang out with my friends." Be specific and show your enthusiasm.

EXAMPLES

"For fun, I like most sports - watching and participating. I am currently on an adult kickball team which is really fun."

"A perfect day? Well, on the weekends, I love to get up, drink my coffee and then head out for exercise. Then I usually have something planned – lunch with a friend, or dinner and a movie. I like some downtime to recharge, but I also recharge by having fun."

29. How do you feel about travel? Late nights? Weekends? Relocation?

STRATEGY

If you absolutely cannot travel, relocate, etc. then you need to let them know. (Do not go into the details.)

If this is a first or second interview and you "prefer" not to travel, etc. - stay positive and let them know you are open to this. If this is a final stage interview, you will need to have further and more specific discussions to determine if it will work for you.

EXAMPLES

"Unfortunately, I cannot work nights. If that is a requirement for this job, then I need to withdraw. But I am very interested in CCC and would hope to be considered for other opportunities."

"I am open to travel and weekend work. As we get further in the process, I would want to know more specifics, but I am open to the possibility."

30. May I ask you to solve a Case Interview problem?

STRATEGY

"Case" Interviews are different than "Behavioral" interviews: they ask you to think through a "case" scenario rather than asking about how you have "behaved" in situations. These interviews are usually known in advance.

The interviewer gives you information on a business issue and asks for your recommendations on how to solve it. You are able/expected to take notes, ask questions and think out loud in solving it. There are many Case Interview videos on major consulting firms' websites; if you know you will encounter them take the time to practice.

EXAMPLES

"Actually, I am familiar with Case Interviews. I would need to borrow some paper to take notes, but yes, that would be fine."

"Certainly. I enjoy the Case interview format and find them interesting."

31. What else should I ask you?

STRATEGY
This is a chance for you to bring up what you have not been able to get across before, or to reiterate strengths and experiences.

EXAMPLES
"Actually, I have not had a chance to tell you about my recent project. I am very excited about it and it lines up well with this job's responsibilities."

"I think you have covered everything very well. But I would like to reiterate my interest in this position and that my skills and accomplishments would serve me well at CCC."

My interview strategy notes:

____

____

____

____

____

____

32. What questions do you have for me?

STRATEGY

Another chance for you to show that you have done your research! Ask strategic questions about the job, company or industry. Have 2 or 3 questions ready before the interview. Do not ask anything about vacations, raises, promotions, etc. Do not ask questions that are answered on the website.

EXAMPLES

"Yes, I noticed recently that most of your competitors have changed their distribution strategy. How does CCC view this change?"

"I understand the initial responsibilities of this position and am ready to take them on. But I wanted to ask about down the road. What would you like to see accomplished, so you feel 150% happy with your hire?"

STEP 4:
Networking &
Your Get-the-Job Action Plan

Networking: The most effective way to get a job

All About Networking
Job Search Networking has its own "good karma" cycle; it's a two-way street and people like being able to help you. And at this point you have done the hard work: you know yourself and what you want, so it's easy for others to help without too much effort on their part.

Approach this critical component as an opportunity to let people know specifics about you, and for you to find out more about them. Keep this in mind, thank your contacts, follow up and help them as you can, and you will be rewarded with strong relationships and good job leads.

Networking Essentials

Respect their Time –
It may take them a little while to respond/get back to you. That's OK; do not take this personally. Keep them on your list so you will follow up. Never mention the "not returned" email or message. Give them a week and then try to re-connect. You may want to try a different mode: email, phone, letter, etc.

The Request –
Polite, to the point, and clear on what you would like: "May I buy you a quick cup of coffee and tell you about my job search?" "May I stop by for 10-15 minutes to drop off my resume/update you/ask your opinion...?" "I am starting a job search and John Smith suggested I contact you. May I stop by for 10 minutes..."

The Meeting –
Keep it specific and focused; respect their time and energy. If they say: "So what can I do for you?" or "We aren't hiring; I'm not sure what I can do for you" you will tell them: "I have started a job search and know that networking is the best way to find a job. I appreciate your time and want to share my background and what I am looking for. Any thoughts you may have, now or in the future, would be appreciated." Remember to respect their time!

The Data-
As you intentionally develop your list of contacts, target companies and jobs/industries, you will need a system to keep organized and proactively focused, not just responding to the latest possibility. Develop your own Excel or Evernote.com system, or use JibberJobber.com, which was designed for the job search.

Networking Actions:

This is much more fun than attending networking events.

Start with your easiest/warmest contacts - - ask for a little of their time; let people know specifically what you are looking for; and strategically grow your contact list so more people will have you in mind when an opportunity presents itself.

Start a list of friendly contacts – don't "qualify" their value to your job search; list them as they come to mind. You will prioritize them later.

___

___

___

___

___

___

___

Networking Follow-up

Definitely send a thank you note and/or email after the meeting, or even after a nice phone call. Hand-written notes are so rare – and very favorably received.

After that, think of ways to keep in touch every 2-3 weeks, so they have positive reminders of you on a regular basis. Most anything clever, nice, current and thoughtful will send a positive reminder of you.

Examples:
"I saw this article and thought of you..."
"I thought of you when I (saw a mutual friend; read an article; your team won; your company was listed in the top...)
"I have updated my resume and wanted to send you a copy..."
"I wanted to follow up to let you know (how my meeting went; the latest on my job search; that I met with ___and she said "hello"...)

Daily networking meetings are encouraged; 2-3 meetings per week are recommended for everyone. They can be quick coffee, breakfast, lunch, drinks, stop-by-the-office, etc. with a close friend; acquaintance; new contact; target; informational interview; networking; friend's parent or co-worker... the benefit is for you to get out, articulate your sales pitch, and have one more person thinking about you.

Take Action:
Develop a Multi-Pronged Strategy

Your list of contacts, target companies and target jobs/industries will help you create multiple job search strategies. The "multi-pronged" aspect will keep things active, even when one area seems to have slowed down.

Take the following information from your Sales Pitch on Page 27.

Industries I am targeting:

____

____

____

____

____

____

Companies I am targeting:

____

____

____

____

____

____

____

Types of Jobs I am targeting:

____

____

____

____

____

____

Your Secret Weapons: The 3-Day Job Search Cycle; Accountability Coach; "Do-able Goals"

Keep in mind these 3 Job Search areas:
1) Networking
2) Target Companies
3) Jobs and Industries
Think of the search in a 3-rotation cycle. Move through *Networking, Companies, Jobs and Industries* to ensure each area is covered on a regular basis.

Accountability Coach
Ask a friend, co-worker, neighbor (just not a family member or significant other - that gets way too sticky!) to serve as your Accountability Coach. Have weekly check-ins, present your progress reports, and re-strategize on networking and opportunities. This will keep you focused, motivated and re-invigorated.

"Do-able Goals for Today;
Do-able Goals for Tomorrow"
Organize yourself around short-term, specific goals to stay focused and productive. As you rotate through the areas and goals, you'll find the job search more interesting and you'll also make great progress.

Job Search Cycle 1: Networking

Today:
Grow your Networking List:
-Add 10-15 names to your Networking List. Do not qualify them; just capture their names for now.

-Sign up for, research and get comfortable with Jibber Jobber (or whatever organizational system you will use) and LinkedIn, a great networking tool.

LinkedIn www.linkedin.com
-Watch one of the video tutorials.

-Establish/re-establish your LinkedIn profile: very professional; similar to your resume (copy and paste and it's done!).

-Start strategically connecting with people to build your network.

-Search under "Companies" for your Targets; look at the people in those lists/any connections in common.

-Join appropriate Groups. Search for specific people.

Jibber Jobber www.jibberjobber.com
-Watch some of the video tutorials.

-Start adding networking names and target companies and notes.

-Schedule "To Dos" and your "Follow up" schedule.

-Print a weekly report to see what you've accomplished and share with your "Accountability Coach."

Day _____ "Do-able Goals"

Today I will:

(Examples: add names to my networking list; research my target companies; email 2 former coworkers; apply for 3 jobs.)

____

____

____

____

____

____

Tomorrow I will:

(Examples: contact 3 people on my networking list; do LinkedIn research on people I know; send 3 emails; update JibberJobber.com)

____

____

____

____

____

____

Job Search Cycle 2: Target Companies

Today:

List 7-10 **target companies** that interest you. You will target them by researching their website for news, articles, press releases, people, job openings, etc. Use Google Finance and other research sites for more information on each company. Target these companies for networking: get to know people who know these companies.

____

____

____

____

____

Add them to Jibber Jobber/your organizational system.

-Go to their Website, research people, products, culture, jobs.

-Use Google Finance/research sites and see what Analysts and Markets say about each.

-Look up each on LinkedIn to view possible contacts. Build up your own LinkedIn contacts.

-Add more names to your Networking List. Select the 5 contacts you are most comfortable with and the action you will take with them (email, call, etc.).

Day _____ "Do-able Goals"

Today I will:

____

____

____

____

____

____

Tomorrow I will:

____

____

____

____

____

____

Job Search Cycle 3:
Target Jobs and Industries

Conduct on-going research into the **target jobs and industries** you are interested in: research Associations and organizations for networking and volunteer opportunities; look for Freelance opportunities; research competitors of your target companies; cross-reference; add names to your networking list; and review staffing companies and job websites.

Warning: Do not spend too much time on staffing companies and job websites. Sign up with several of the staffing companies that work in your field in your area; they may contact you about opportunities. Set a timer to review job websites: give yourself 10-15 minutes to search for jobs, companies and apply; then get back on Plan. The job board websites are not likely to give you the Get-the-Job Action Plan results - but they are very likely to take up a lot of time and energy - so stay strategic!

Today:
-Research more information sources: Local business emails; Chamber of Commerce; young professionals' groups; industry or job specific groups; Industry/Association newsletters/websites.

-Call or email your first 5 contacts and set up brief meetings.

-Jibber Jobber contact updates

-LinkedIn contact building

Day ____ "Do-able Goals"

Today I will:

____

____

____

____

____

____

Tomorrow I will:

____

____

____

____

____

____

CONGRATULATIONS – You are Ready!

You know yourself, your values, strengths, and abilities.

____

____

____

You are focused on jobs, companies, and industries.

____

____

____

Your resume and cover letters are ready.

Your interview skills are polished and perfected.

You have your own Sales Pitch/Overview.

____

____

____

You understand and have started Networking.

____

____

____

Your Get-the-Job Action Plan works!

Keep up the good work. To keep the habit and your momentum, continue your "Do-able Goals."

Day ___ "Do-able Goals"

Today I will:

____

____

____

____

Tomorrow I will:

____

____

____

____

Day ____ "Do-able Goals"

Today I will:

____

____

____

____

Tomorrow I will:

____

____

____

Throughout your job search,
Make this your Mantra:

Keep Myself: Focused and Specific

-Keep Myself Focused:
On My Targets.
-Keep Myself Specific:
About My Skills, Target Companies, Jobs.

Build My Network: Deep and Wide

-Build My Network Deep:
Contact Multiple People in My Targets.
-Build My Network Wide:
Seek Contacts Outside of My Natural Group.

About The Author

Terry Patrick Walton is founder of My Career Catapult: The How-to-Find-a-Job website with your own Personal Coach providing job search coaching, resumes, interview skills, and career strategies. It was acquired by ePropelr.com* in 2014. She recently founded 20sEmpowered, a website, blog and resource for career, life and living ideas designed to Power the Potential of 20-Somethings.

Terry's background includes Partner and Consultant with Heidrick & Struggles, an international executive search firm, and Manager of College Recruiting for First Union Florida. Her degree in Psychology from the University of North Carolina-Chapel Hill, Myers-Briggs (MBTI) Certification, and on-going interests in people, business, and strategy have provided valuable knowledge and experience as she focuses on the behavioral science and economics of work and life.

* **ePropler.com** has Job Search Coaching, Resumes, and Interview practice to complement ***Yes!* The Job is Mine**. For a 10% discount on ePropelr.com, use the code: CATAPULTME!